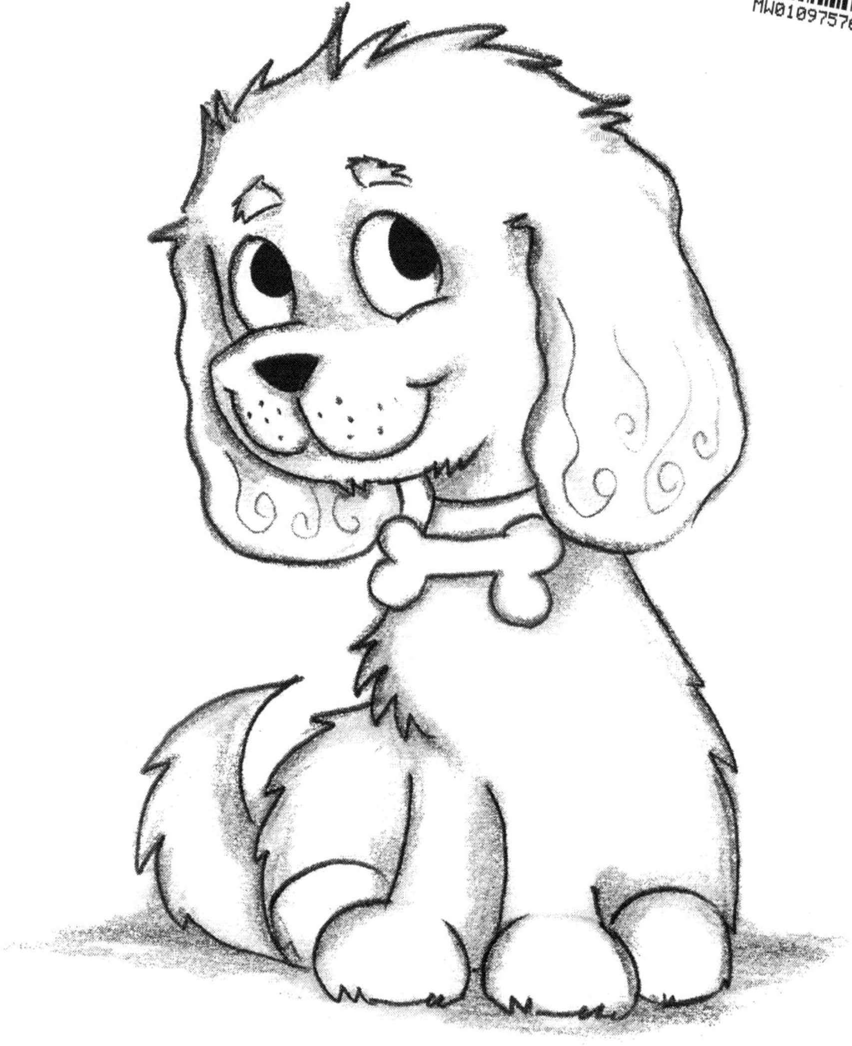

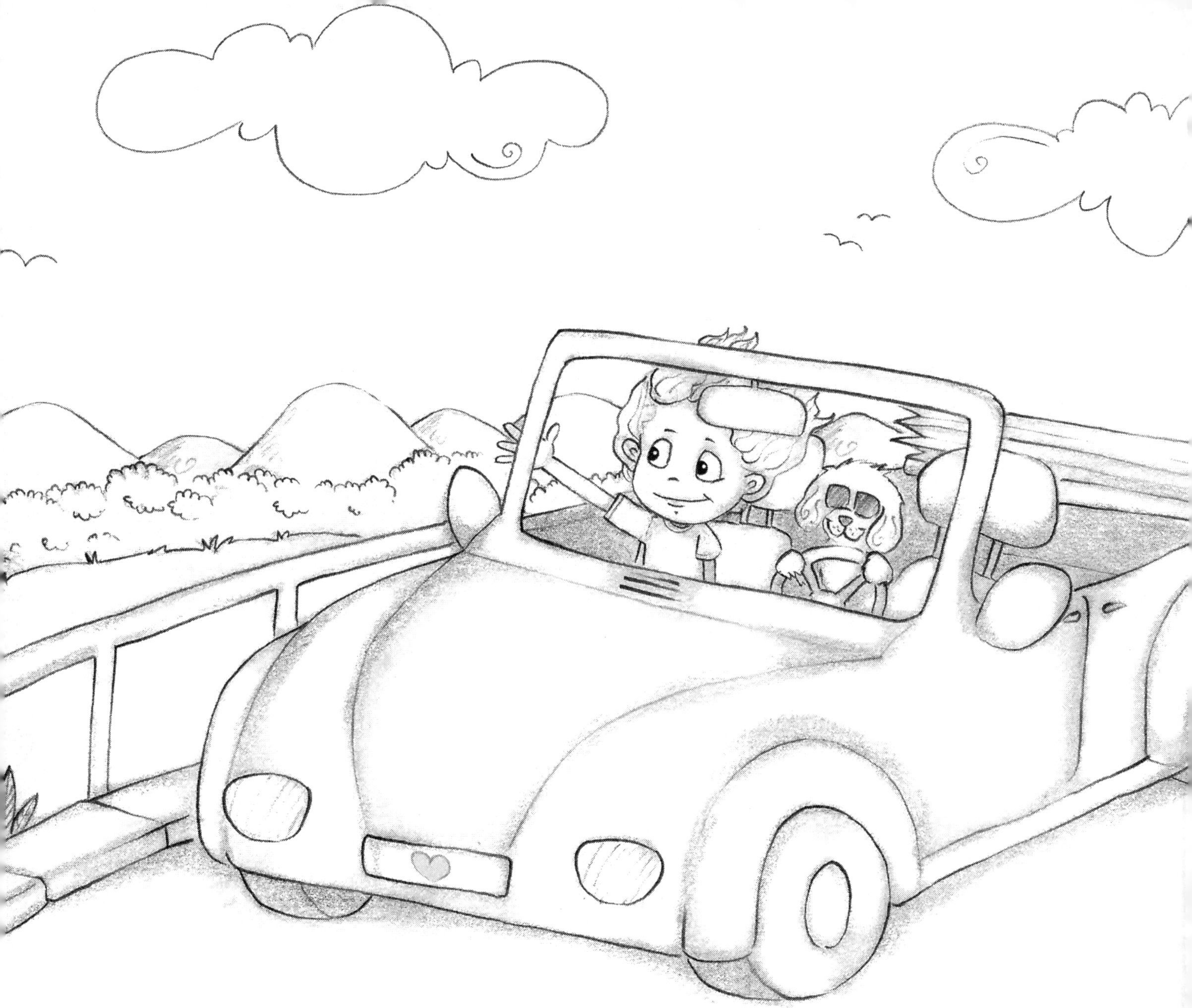

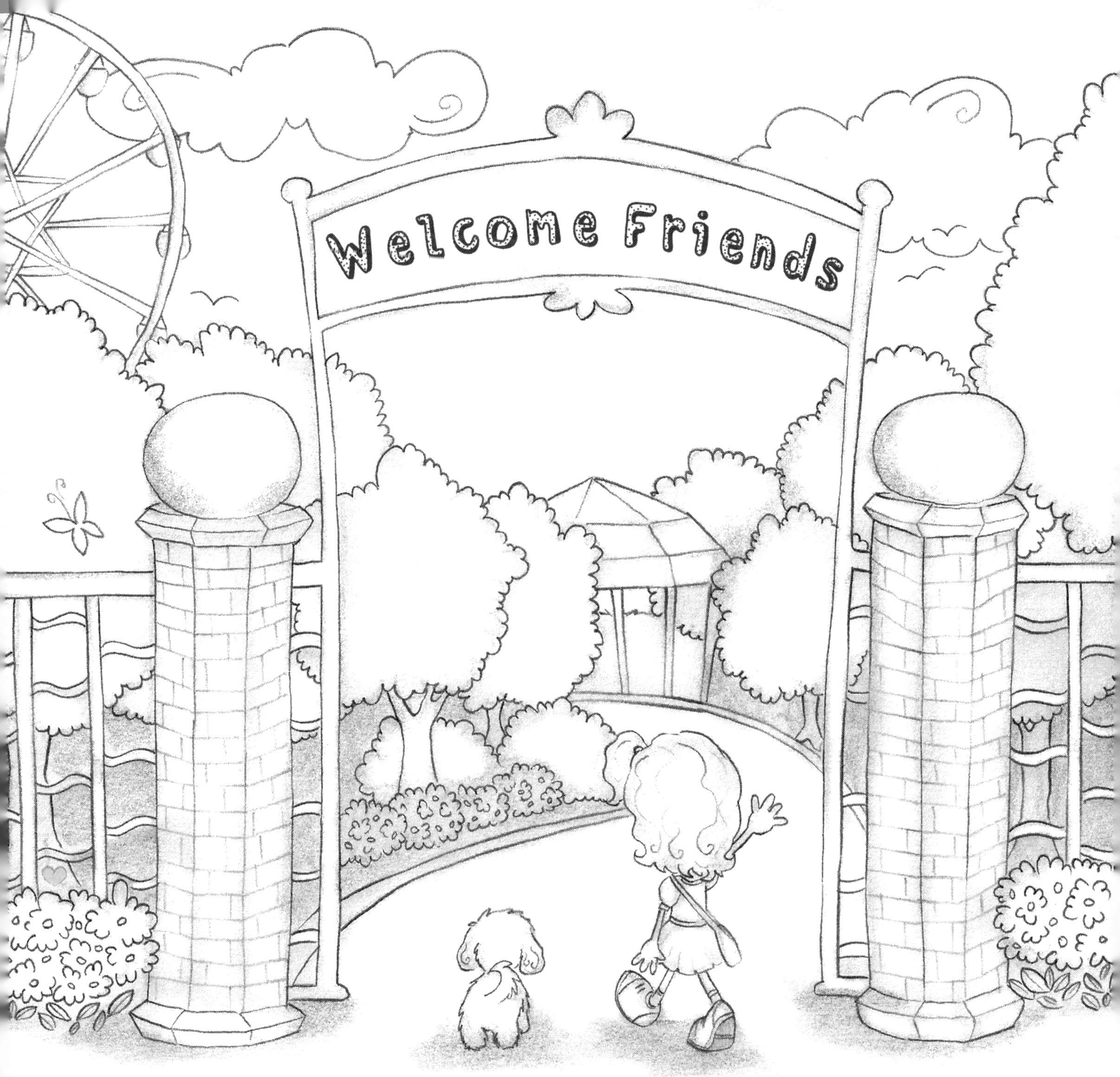
Welcome Friends

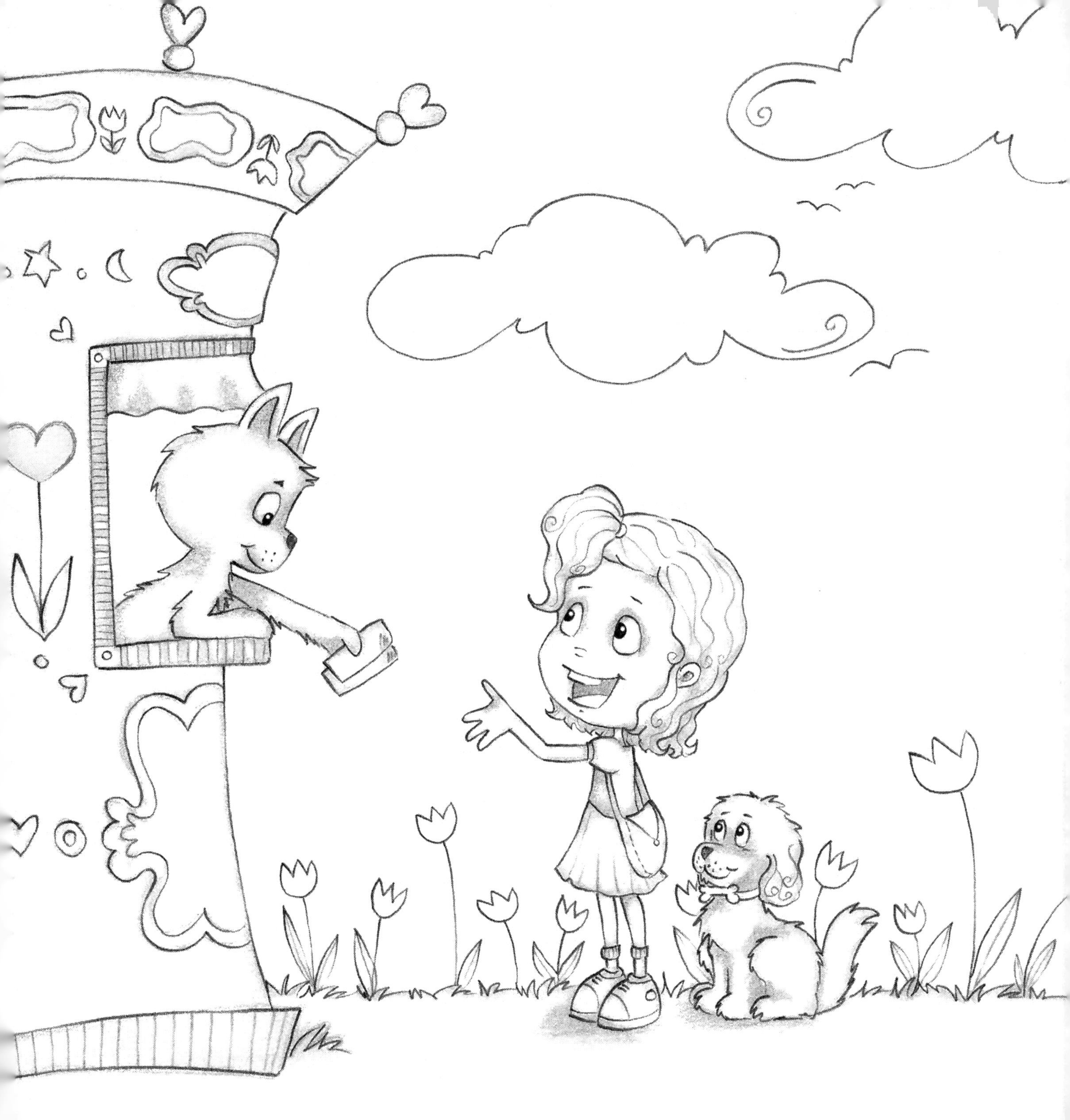

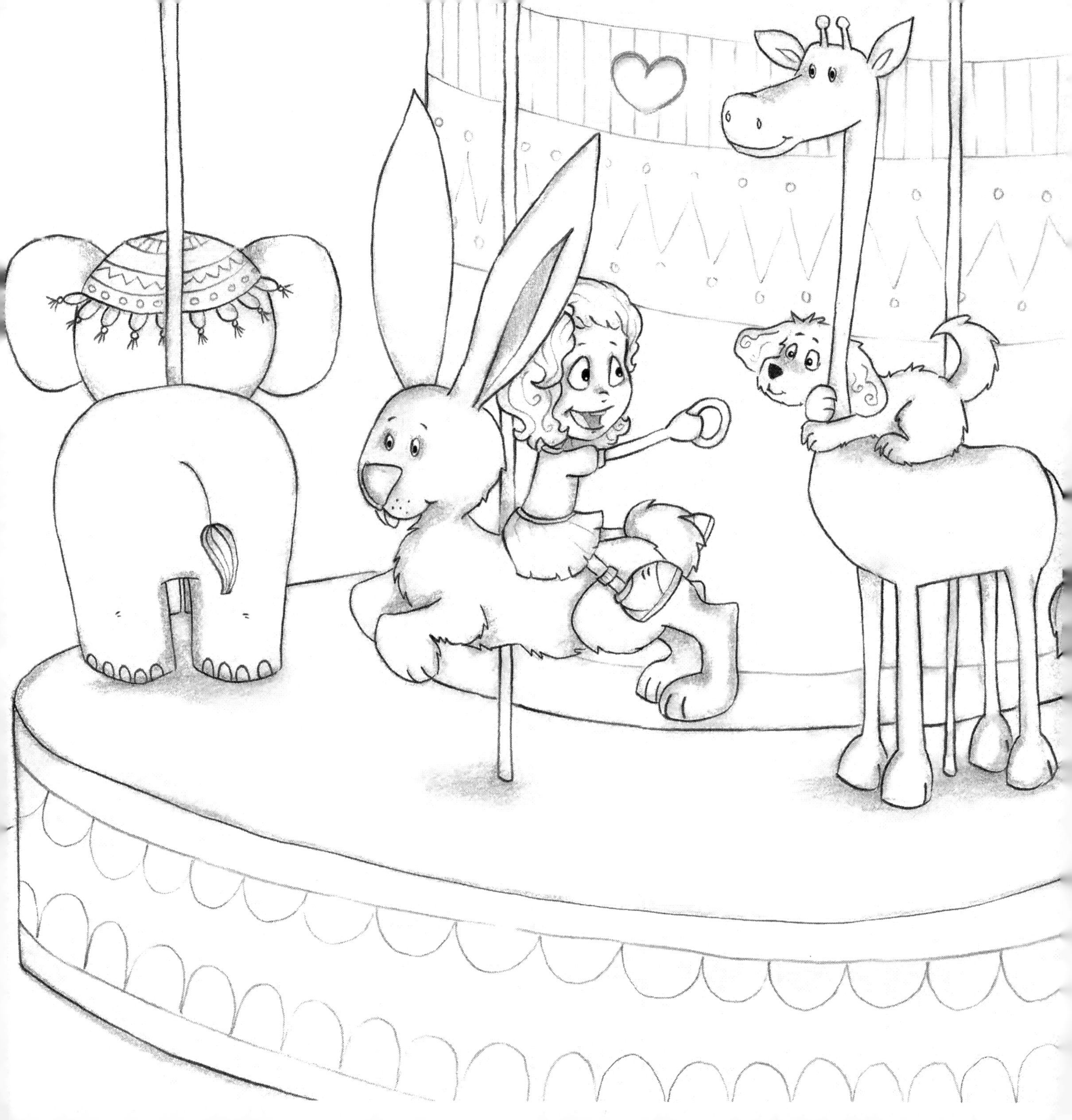

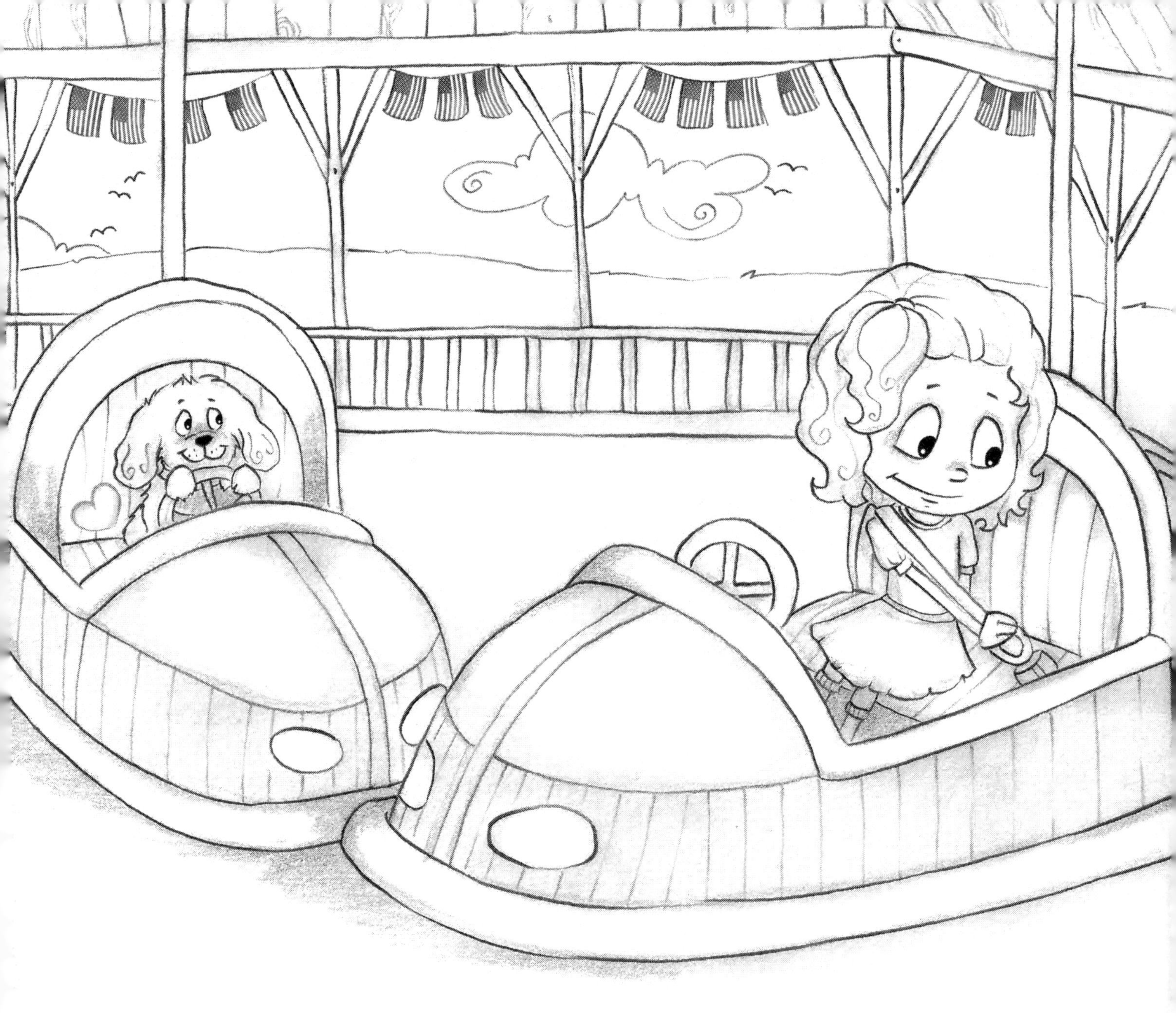

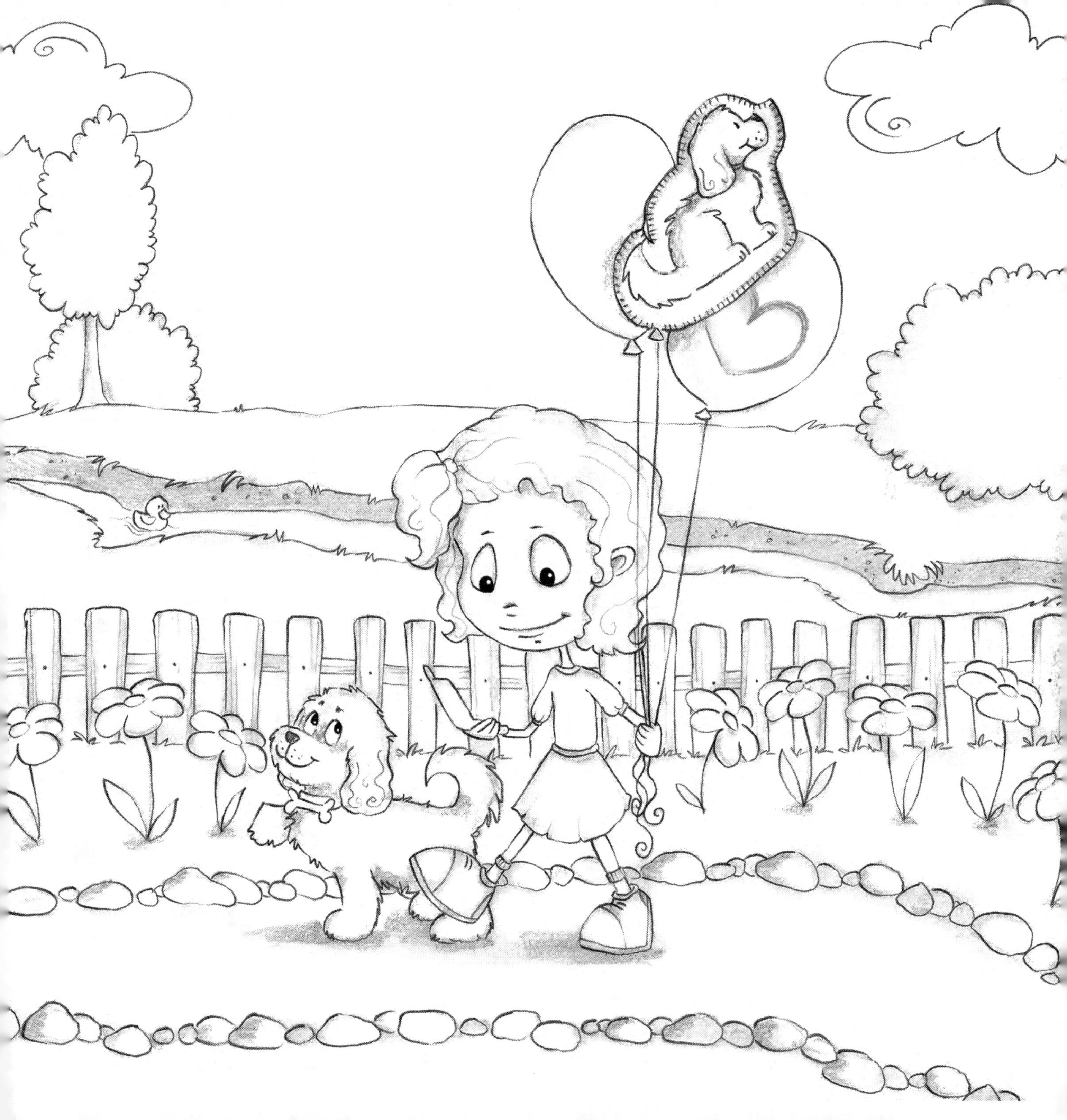

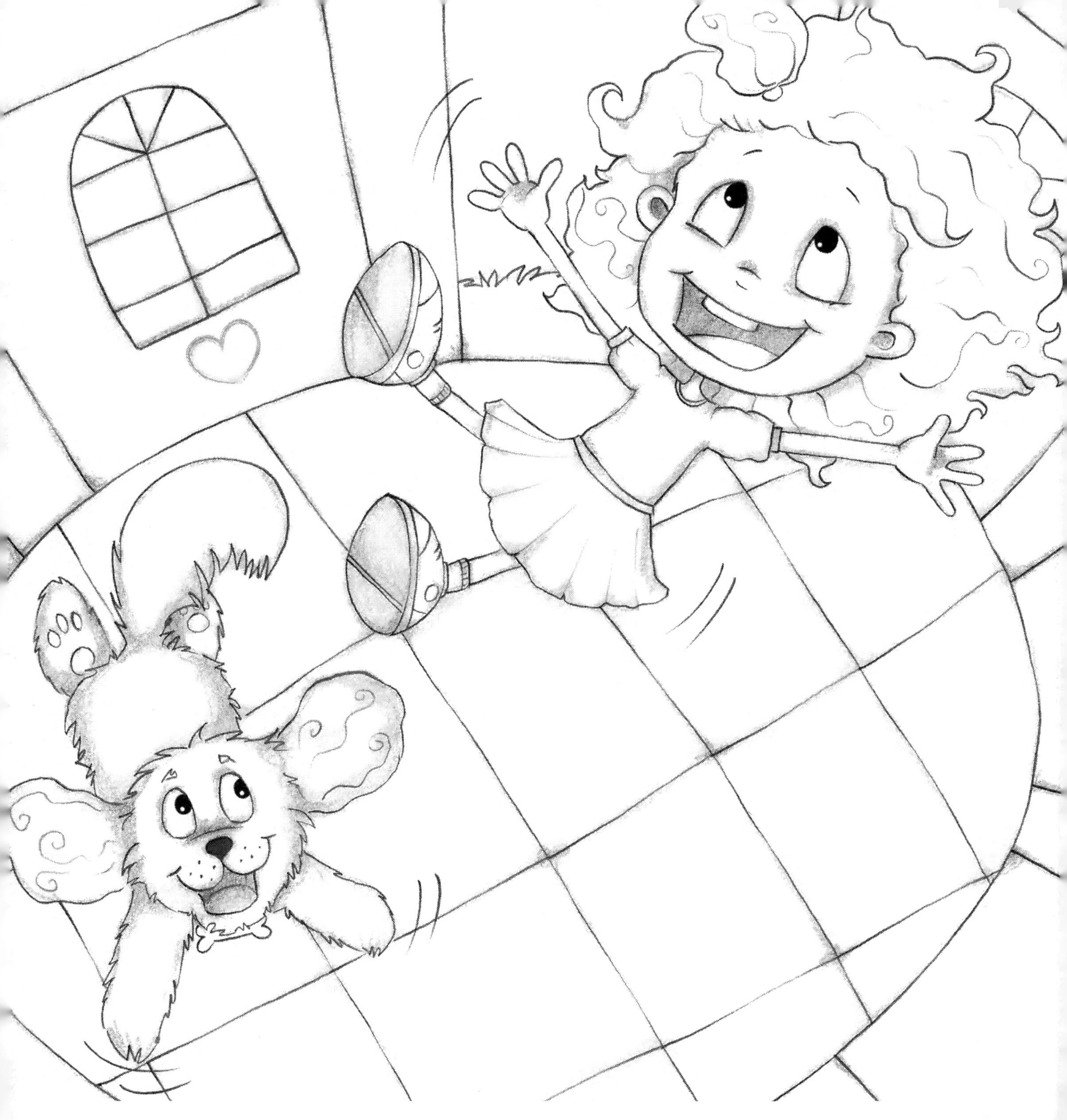

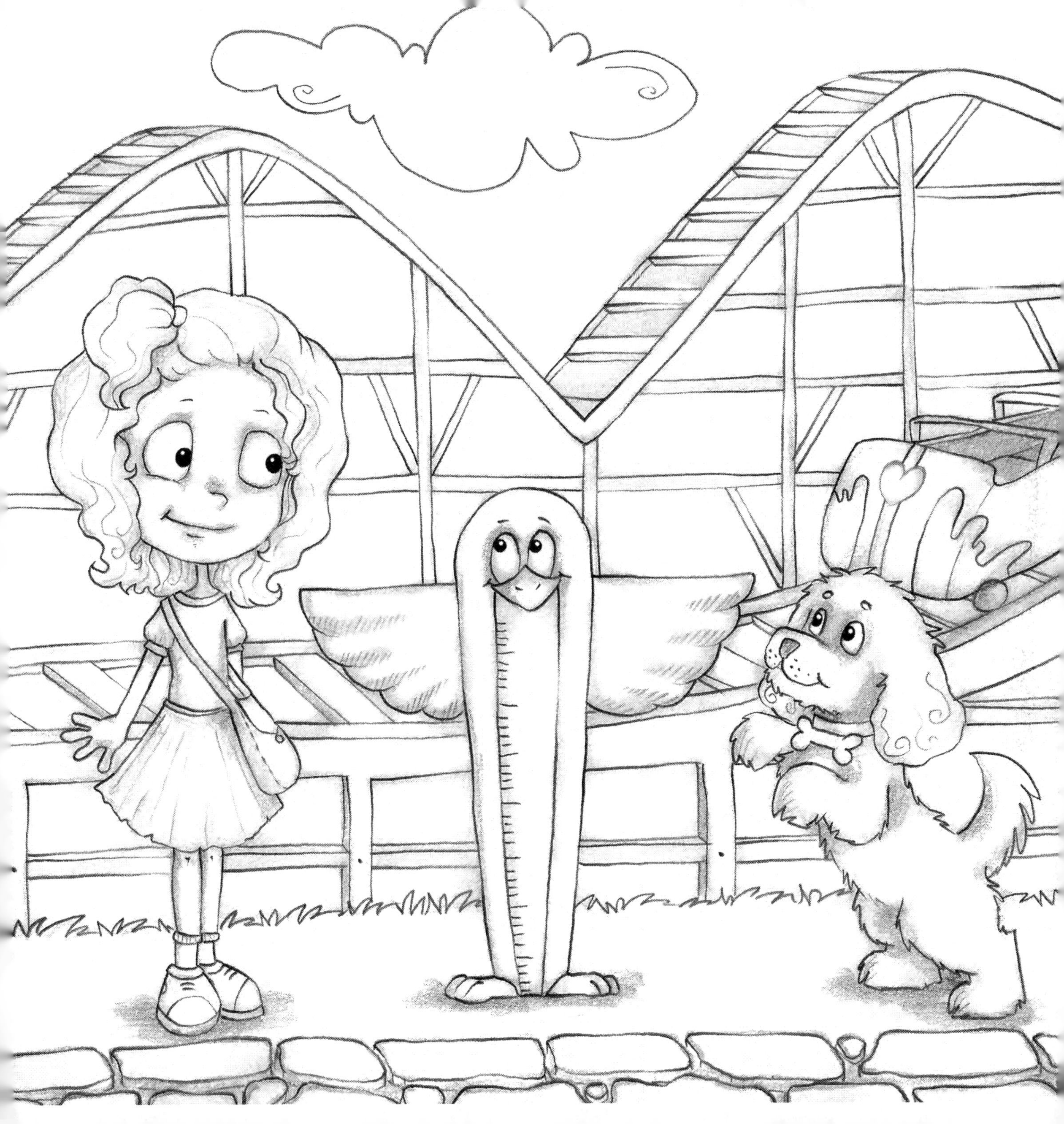

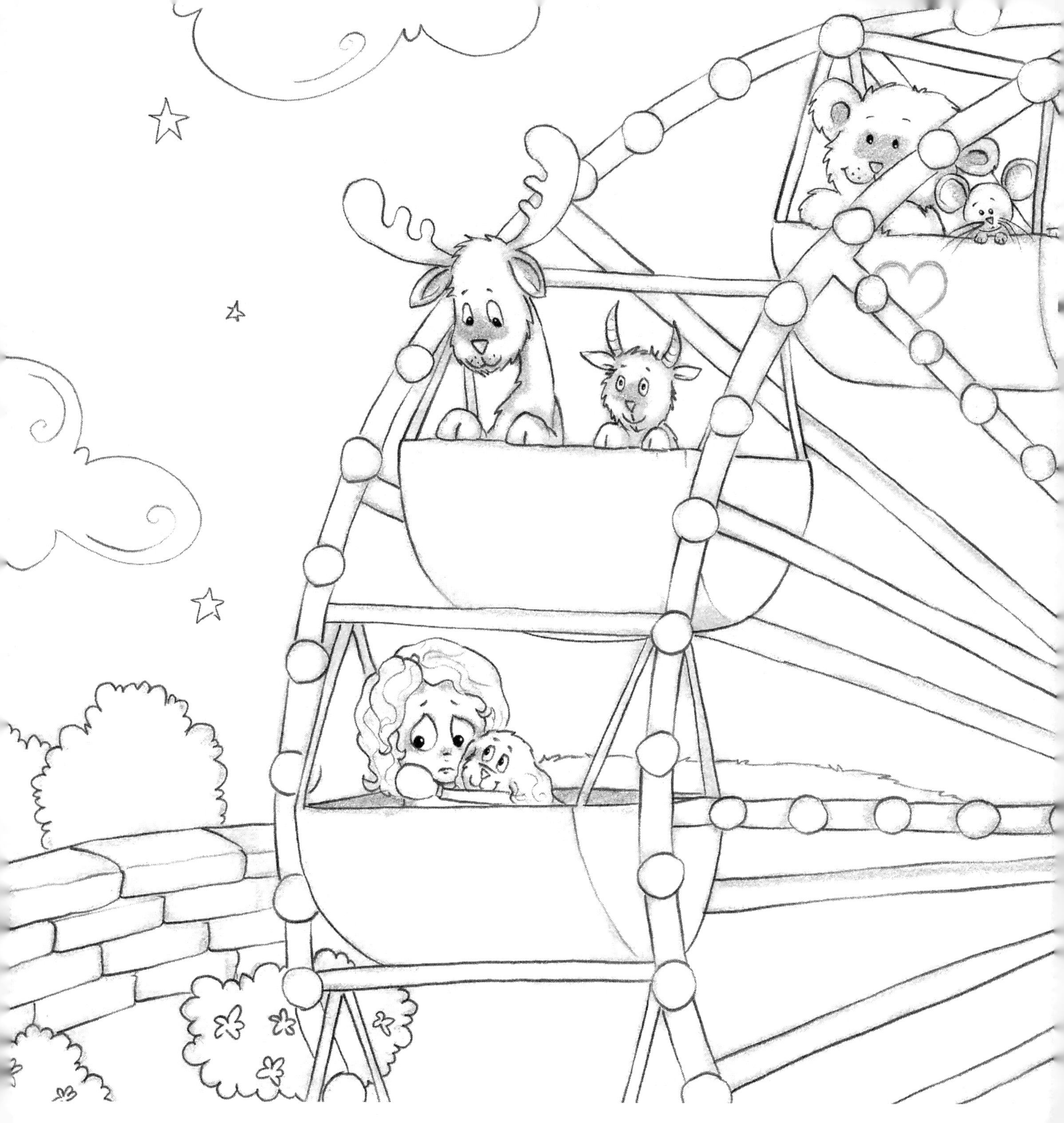

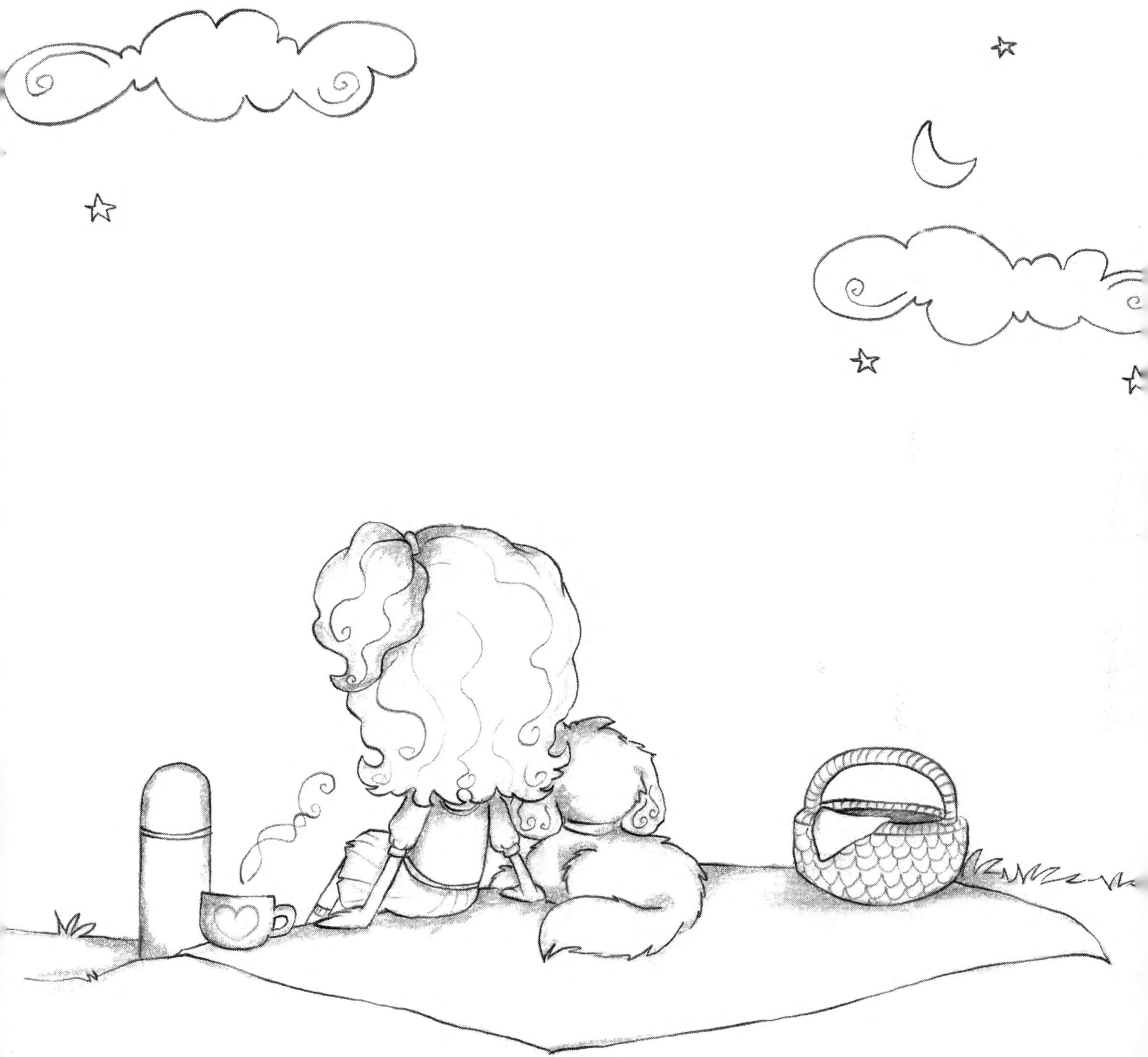

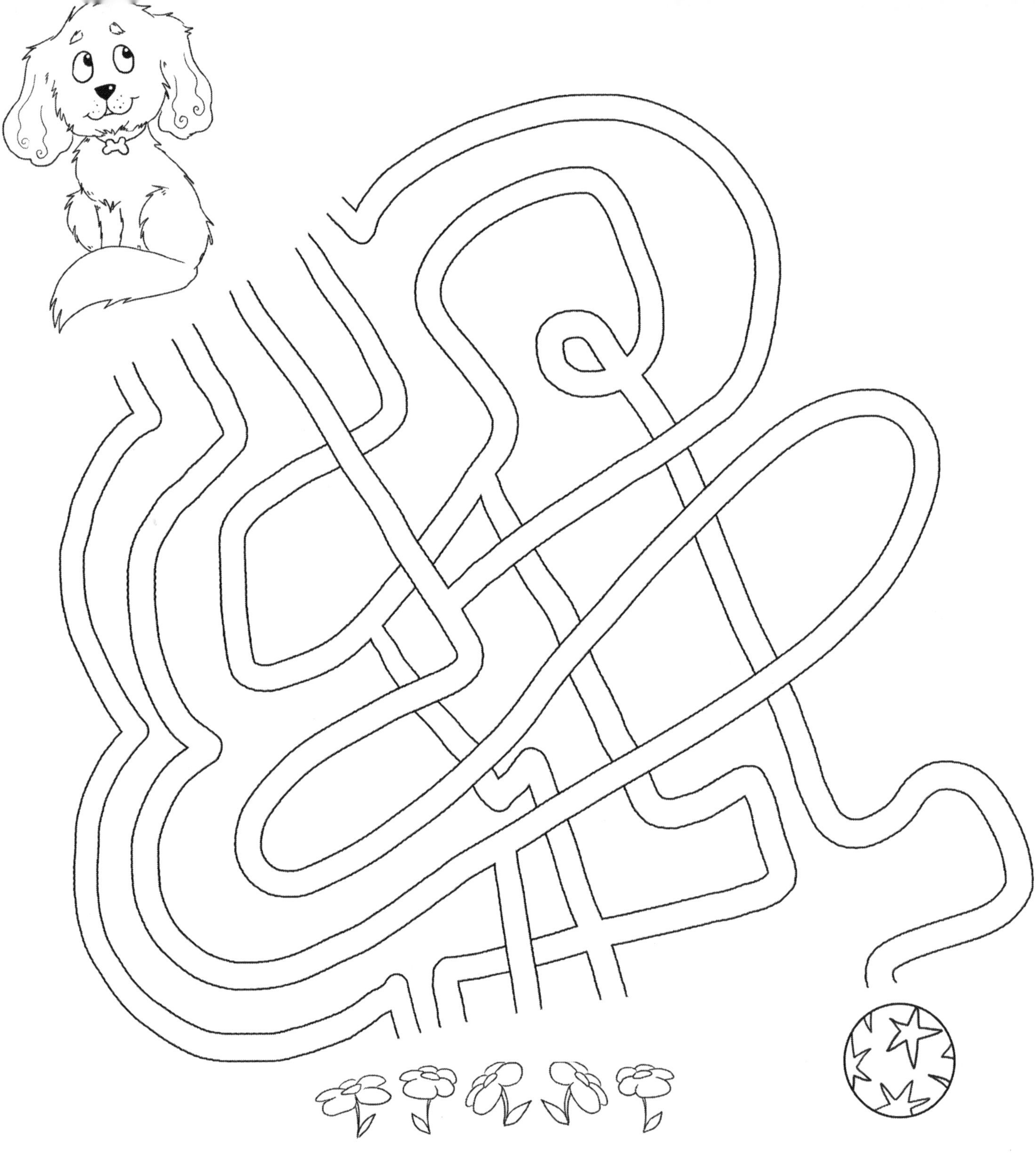

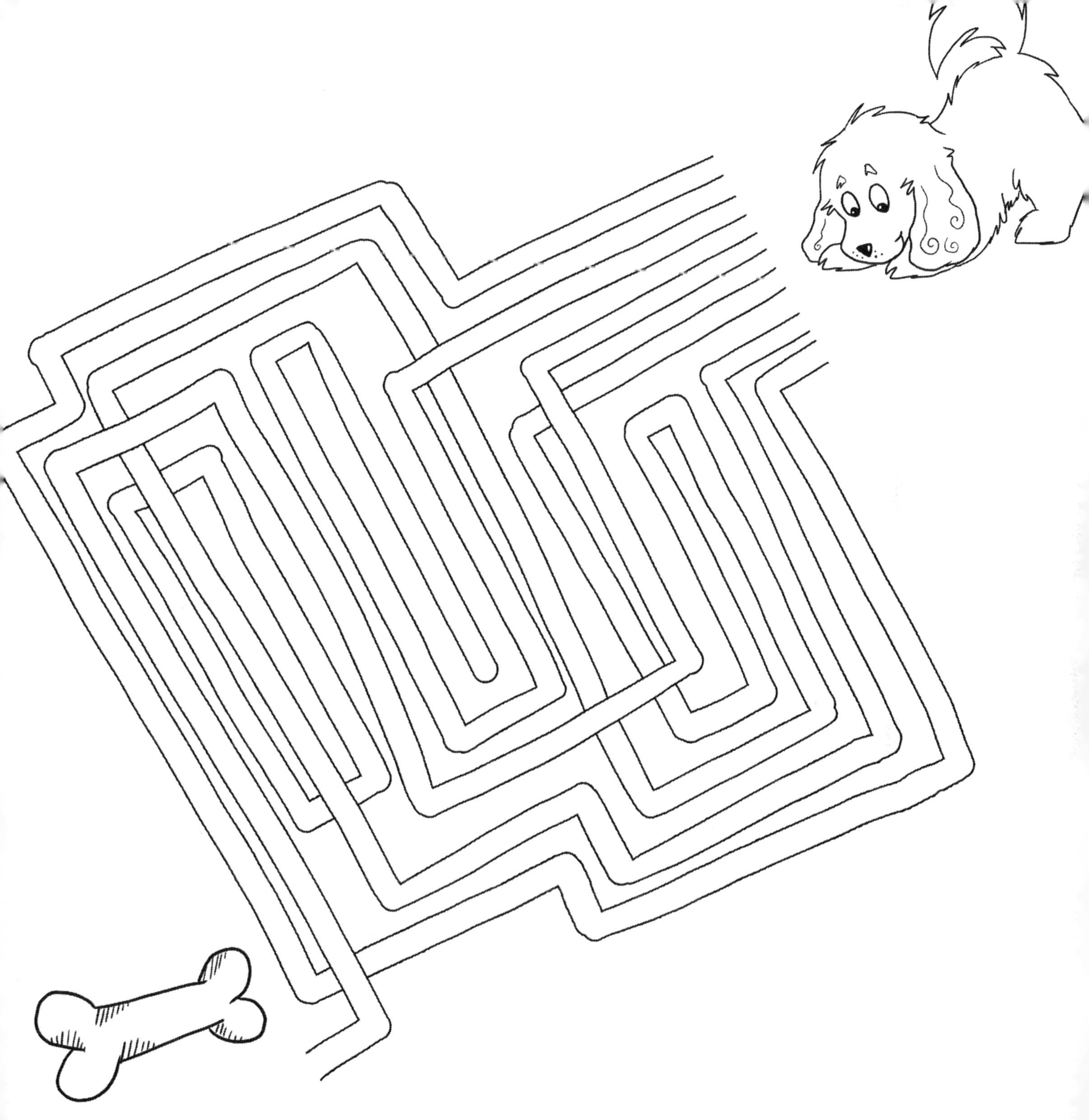

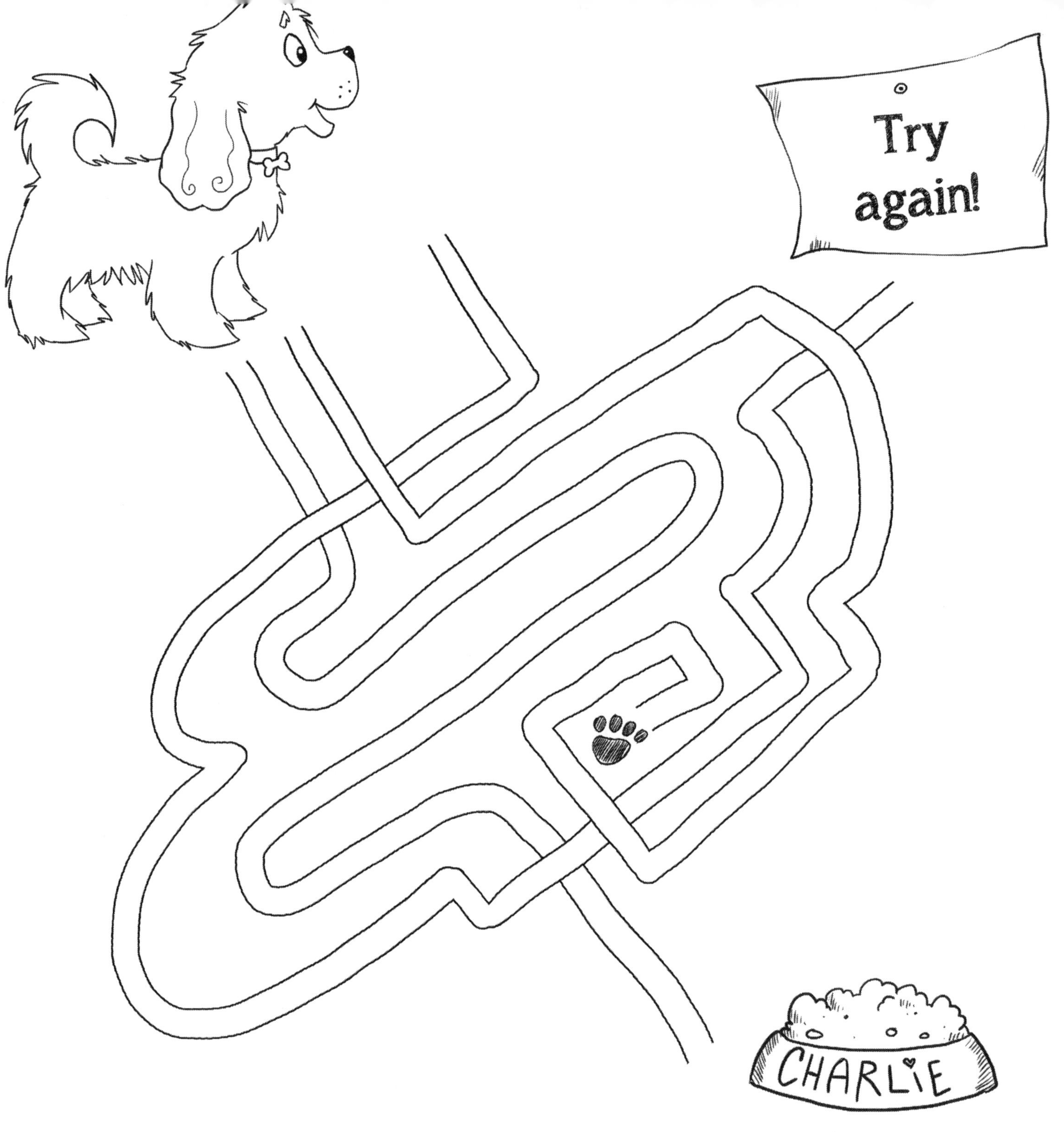
Try again!
CHARLIE

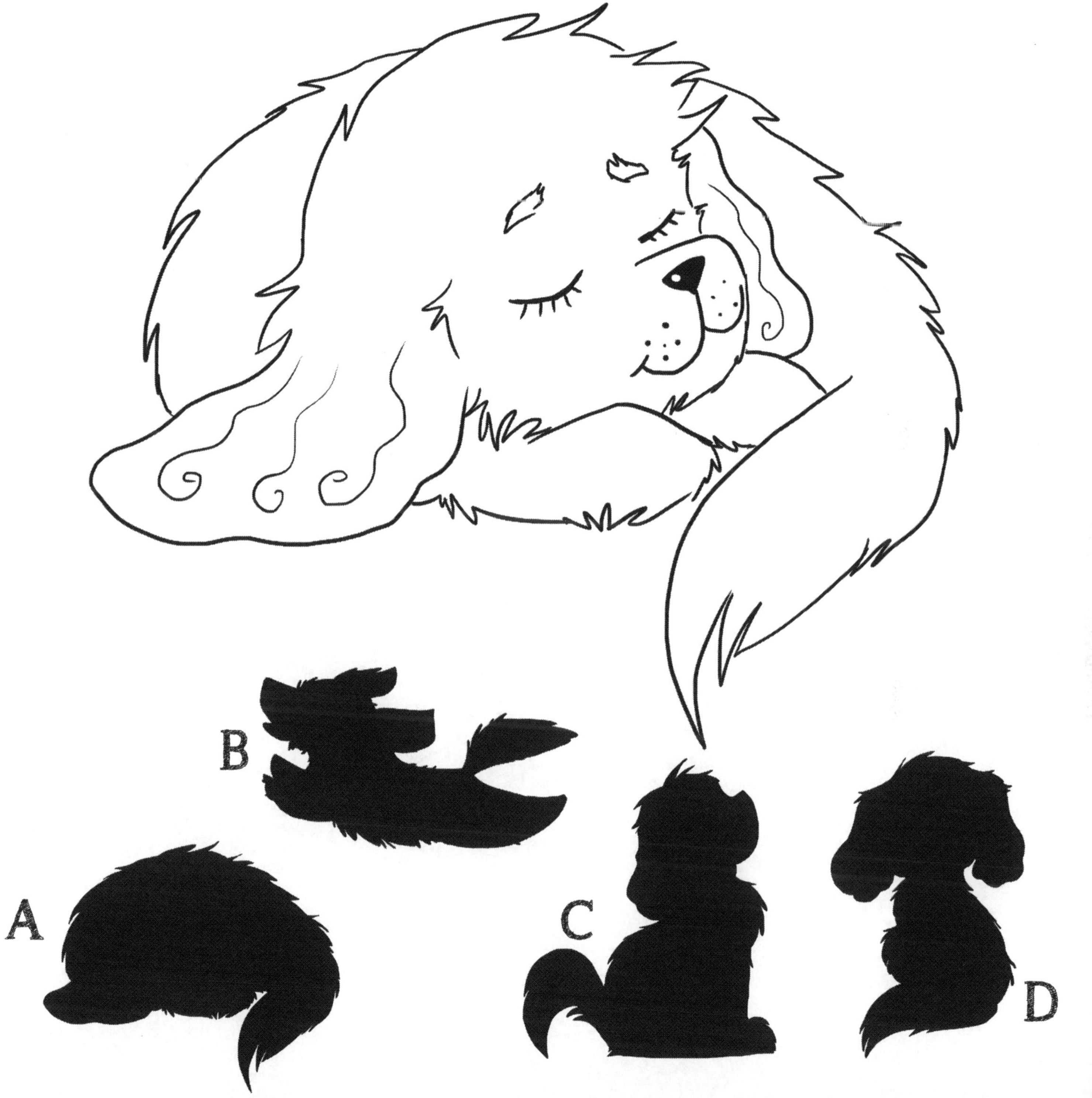

B
A
C
D

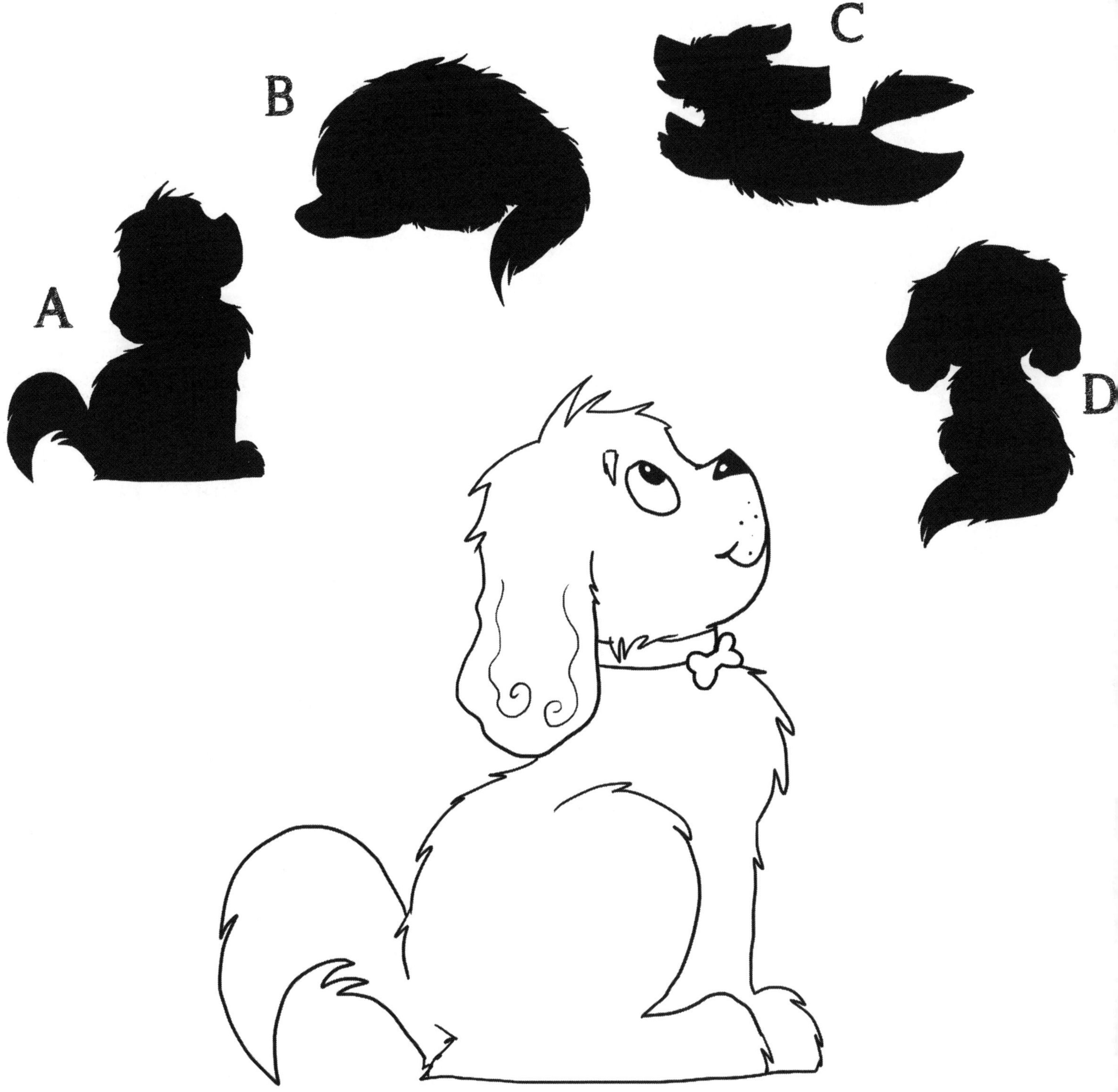
A
B
C
D

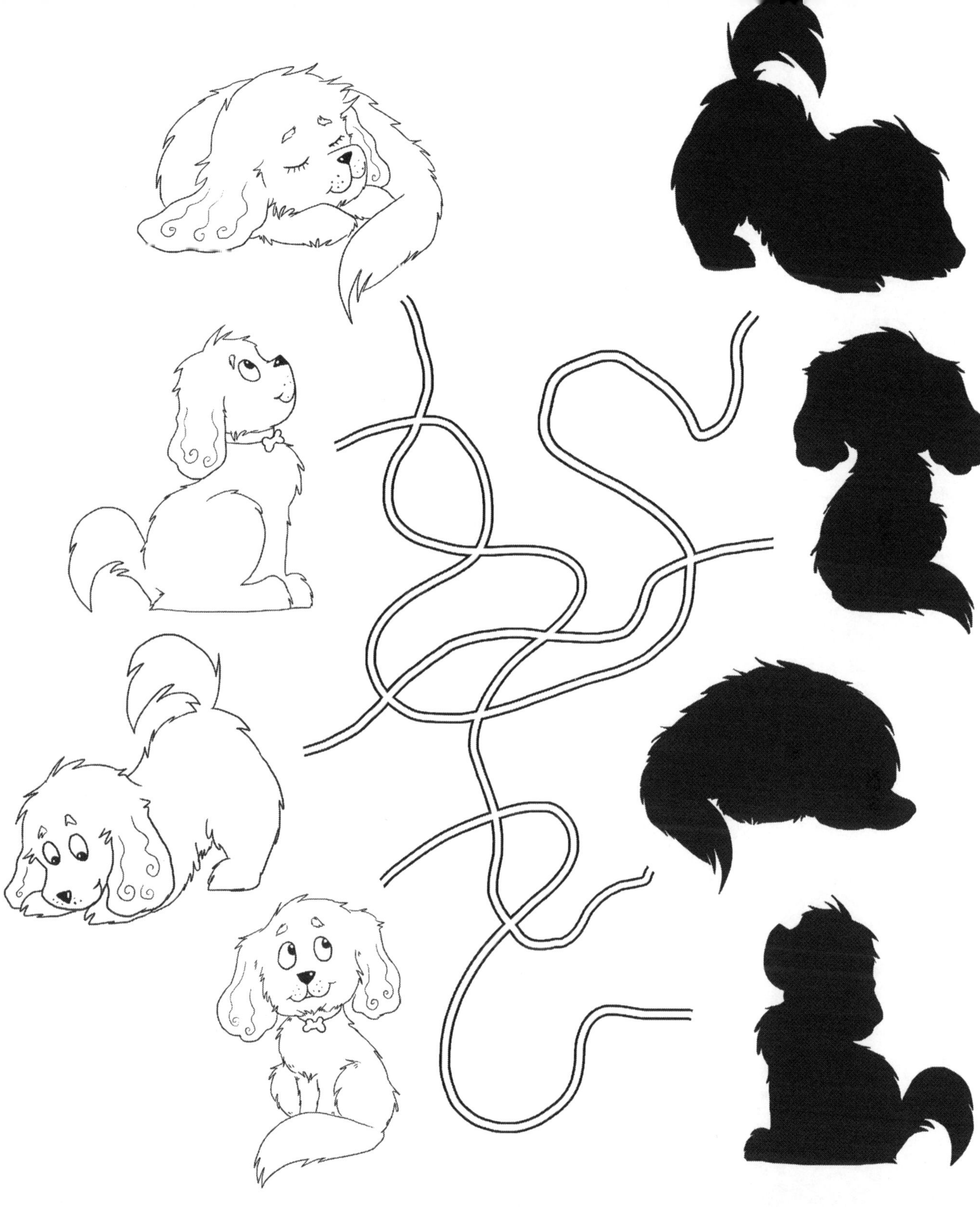

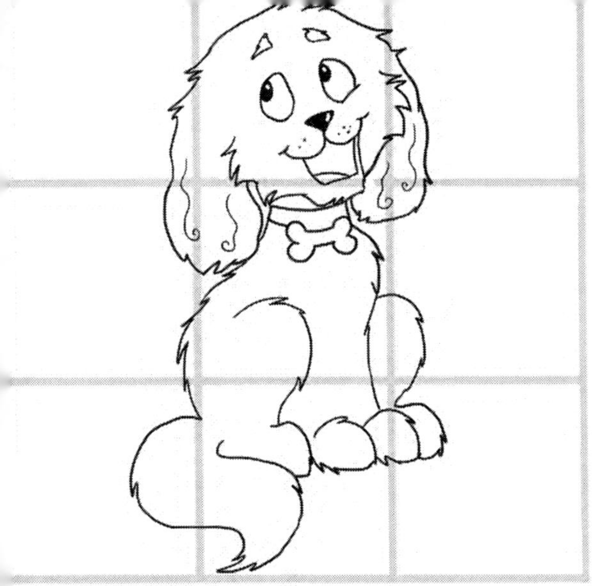

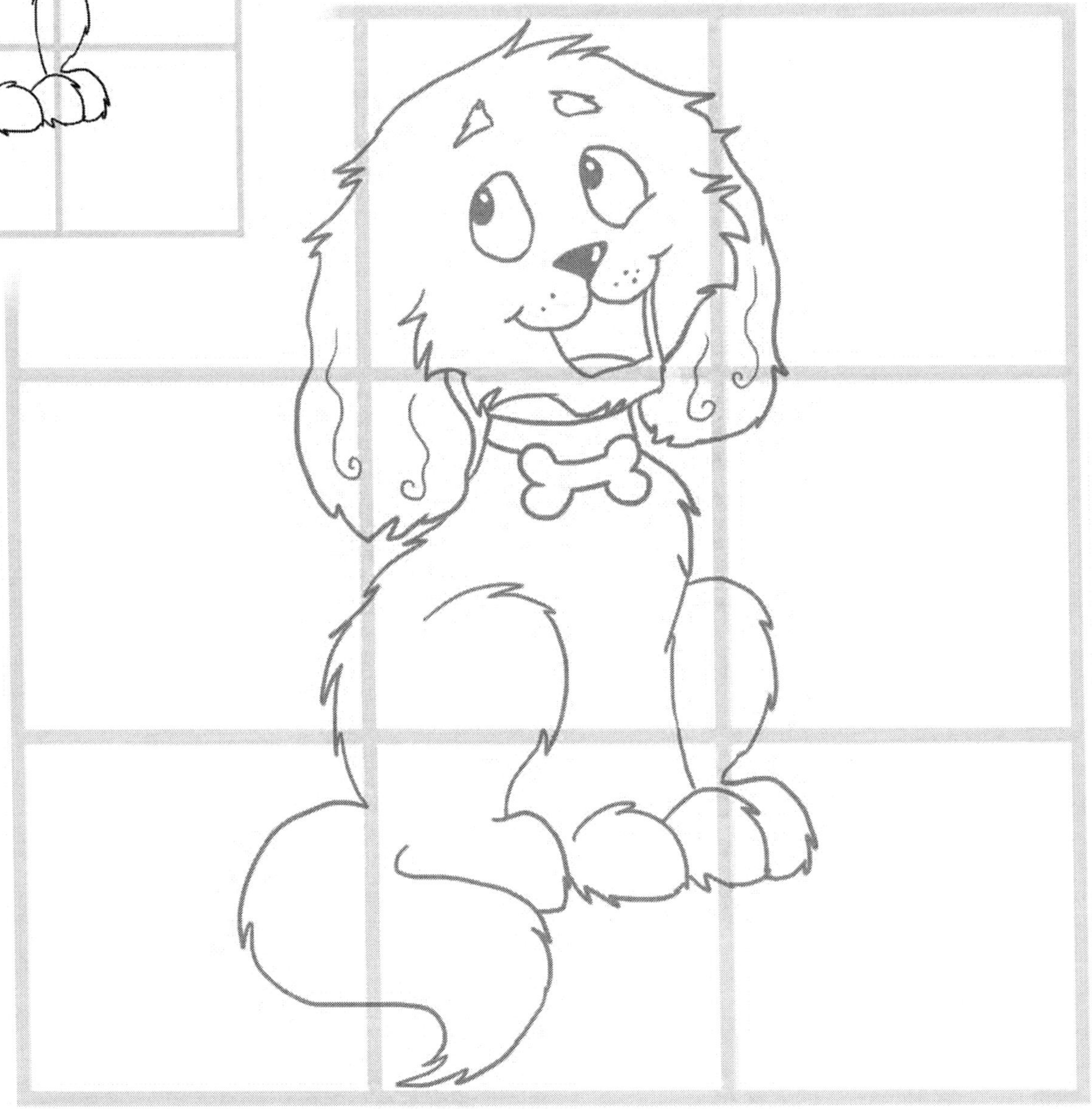

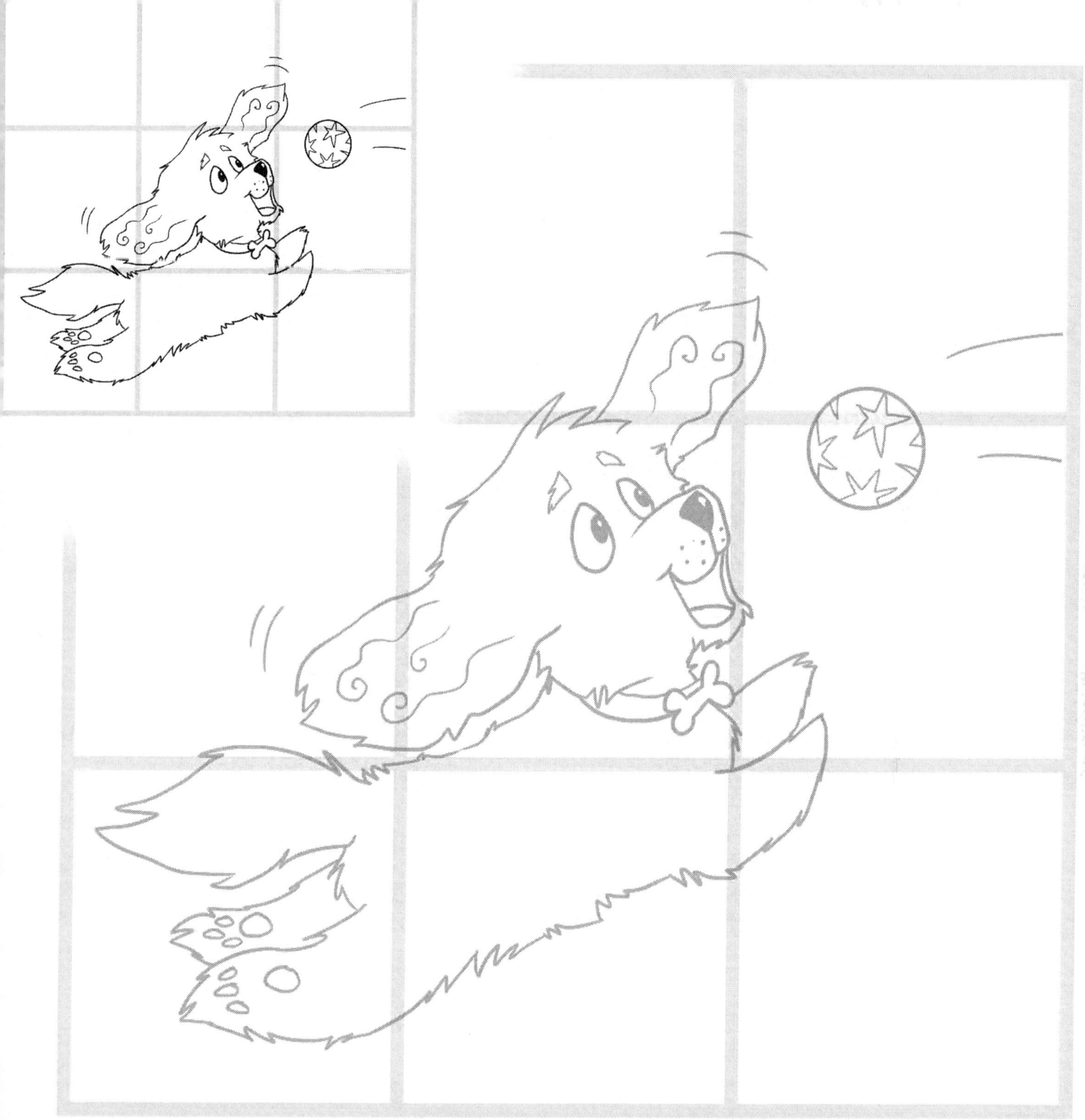

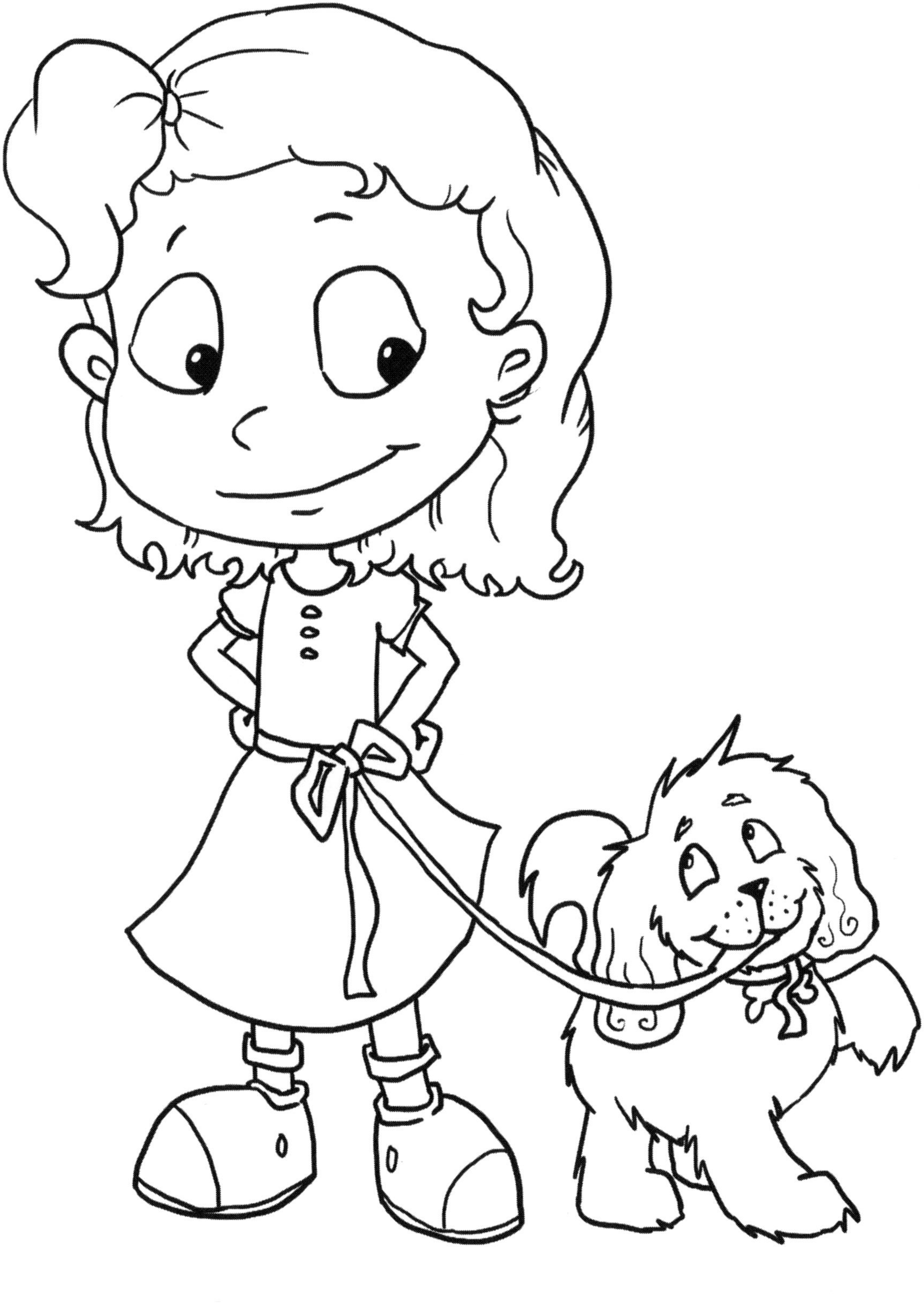

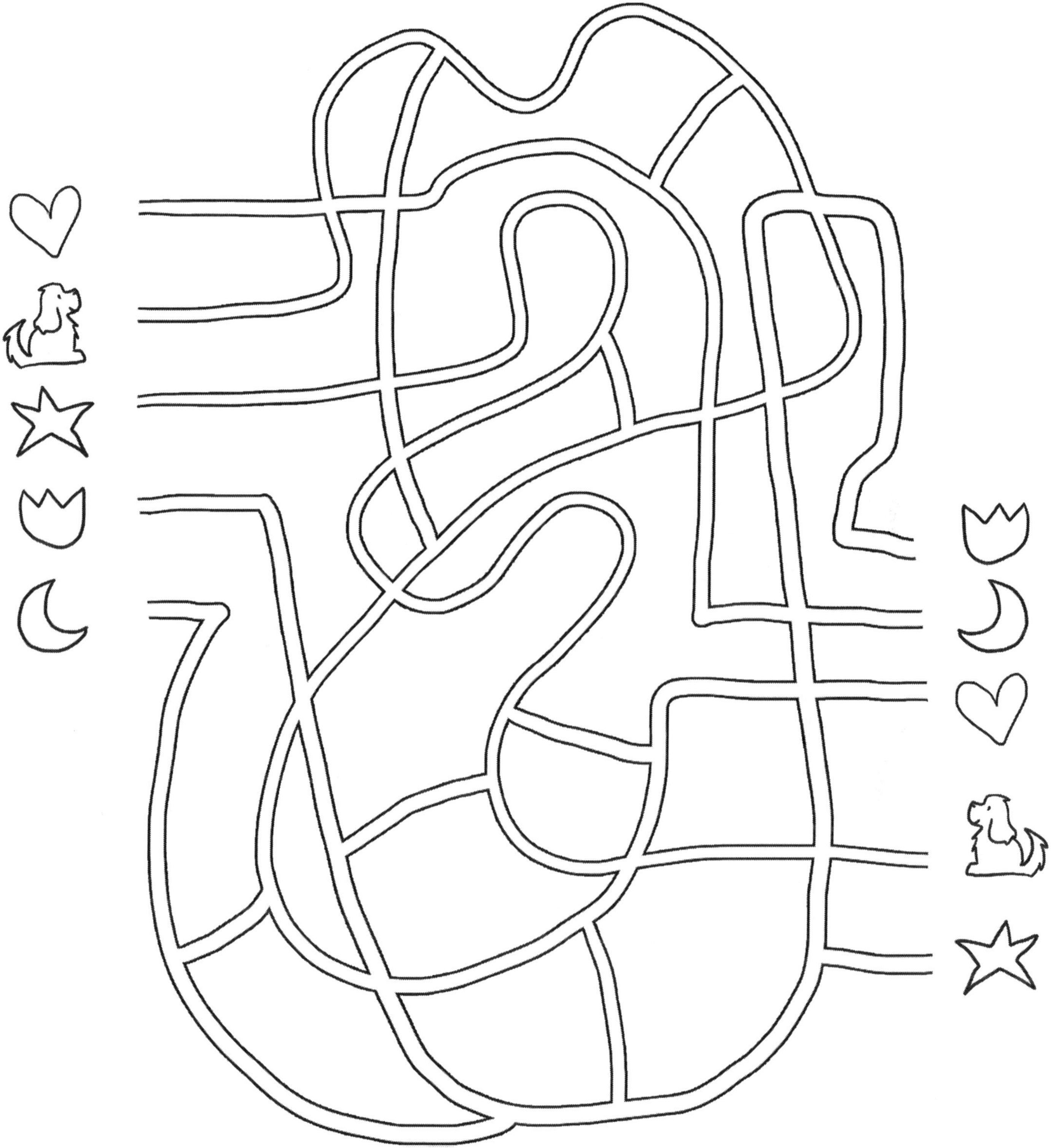

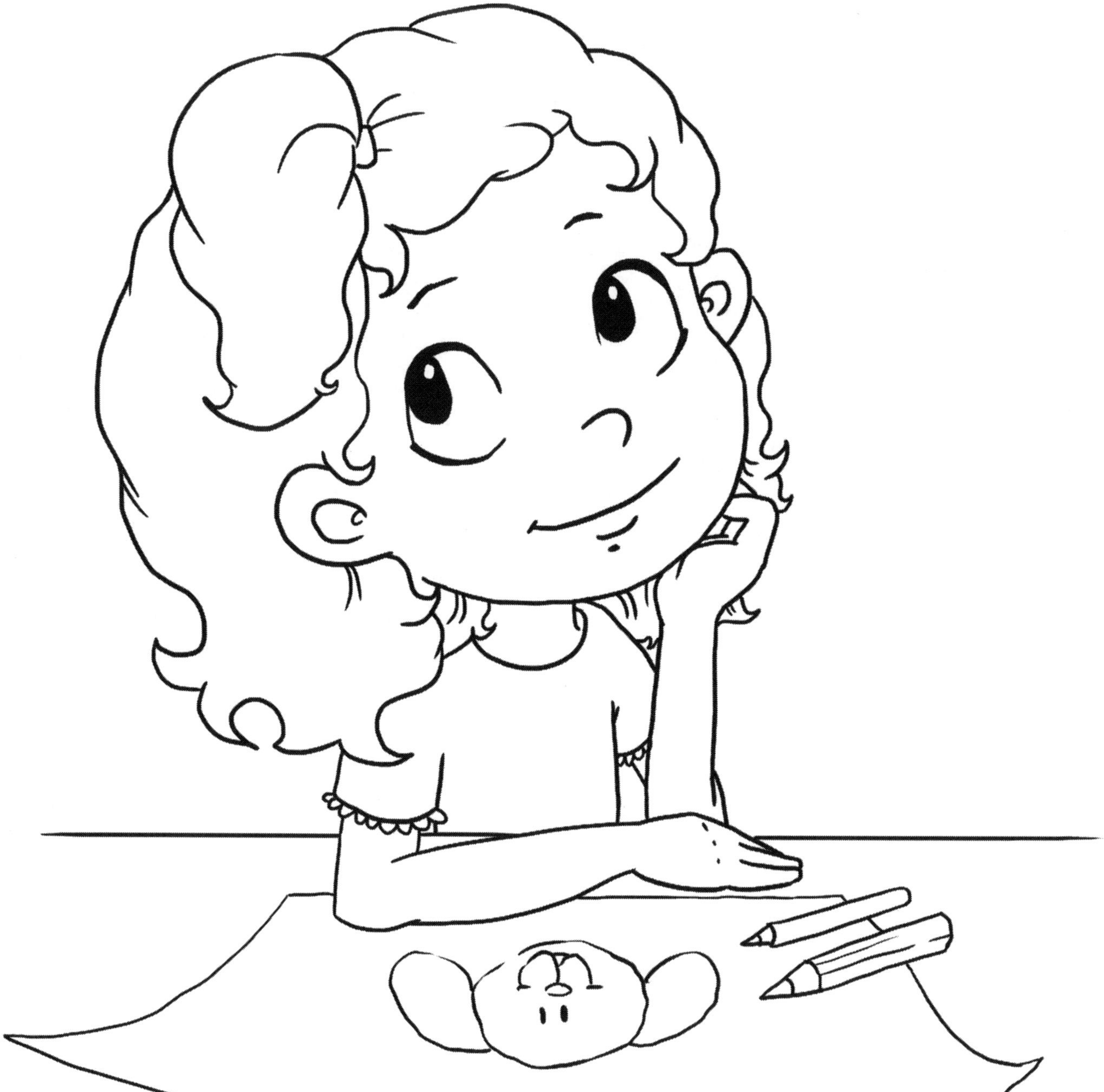

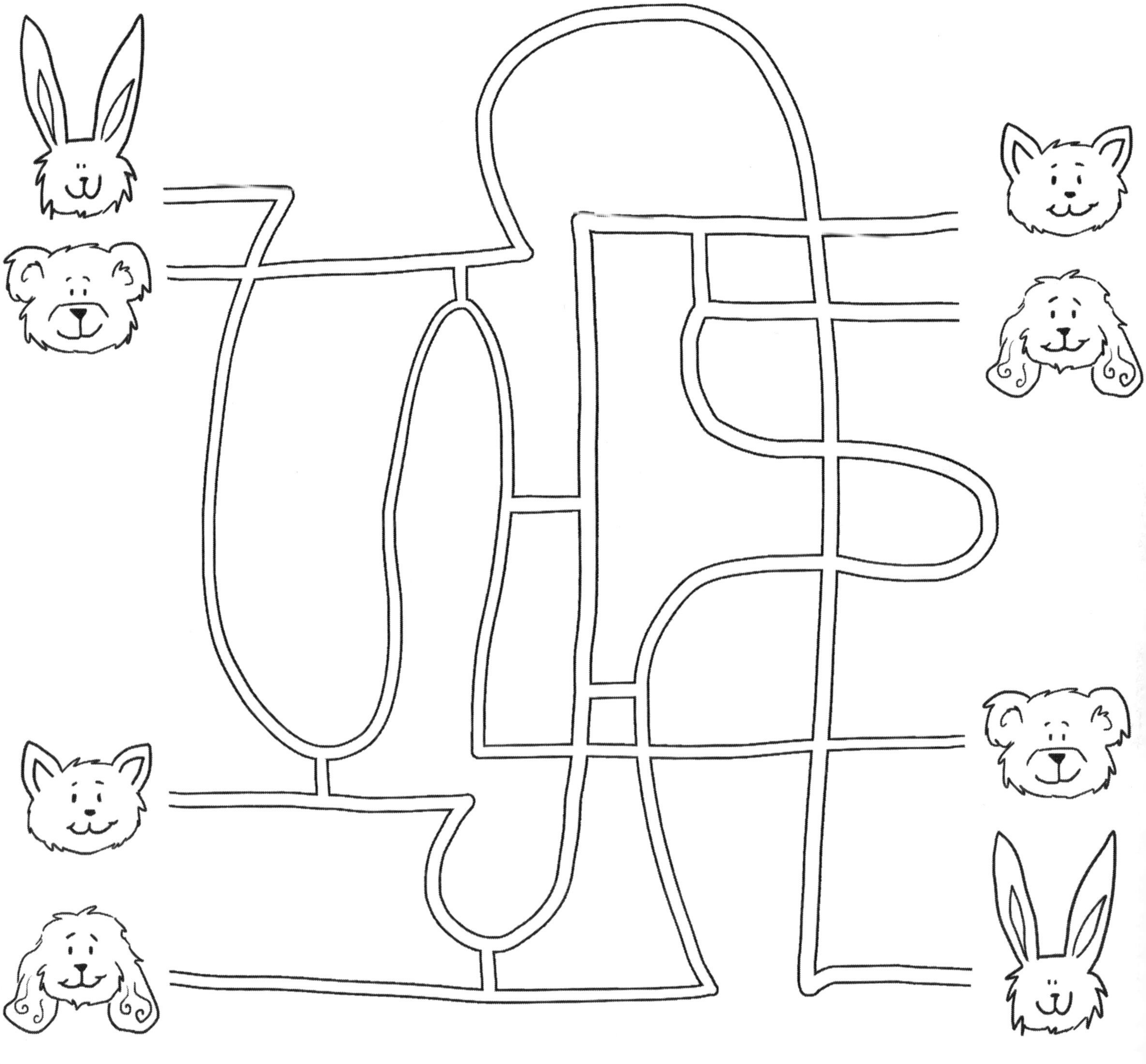

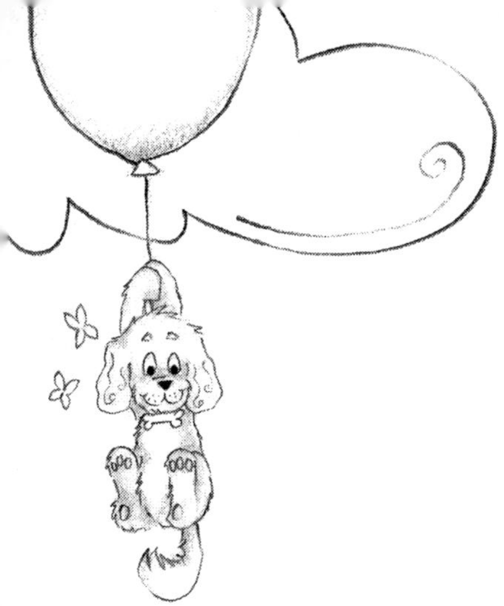

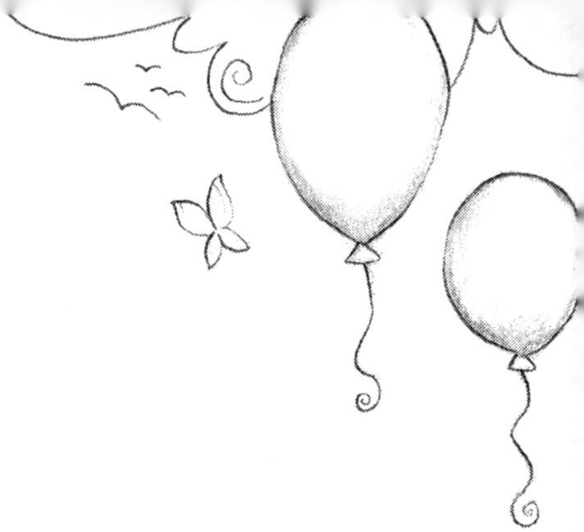

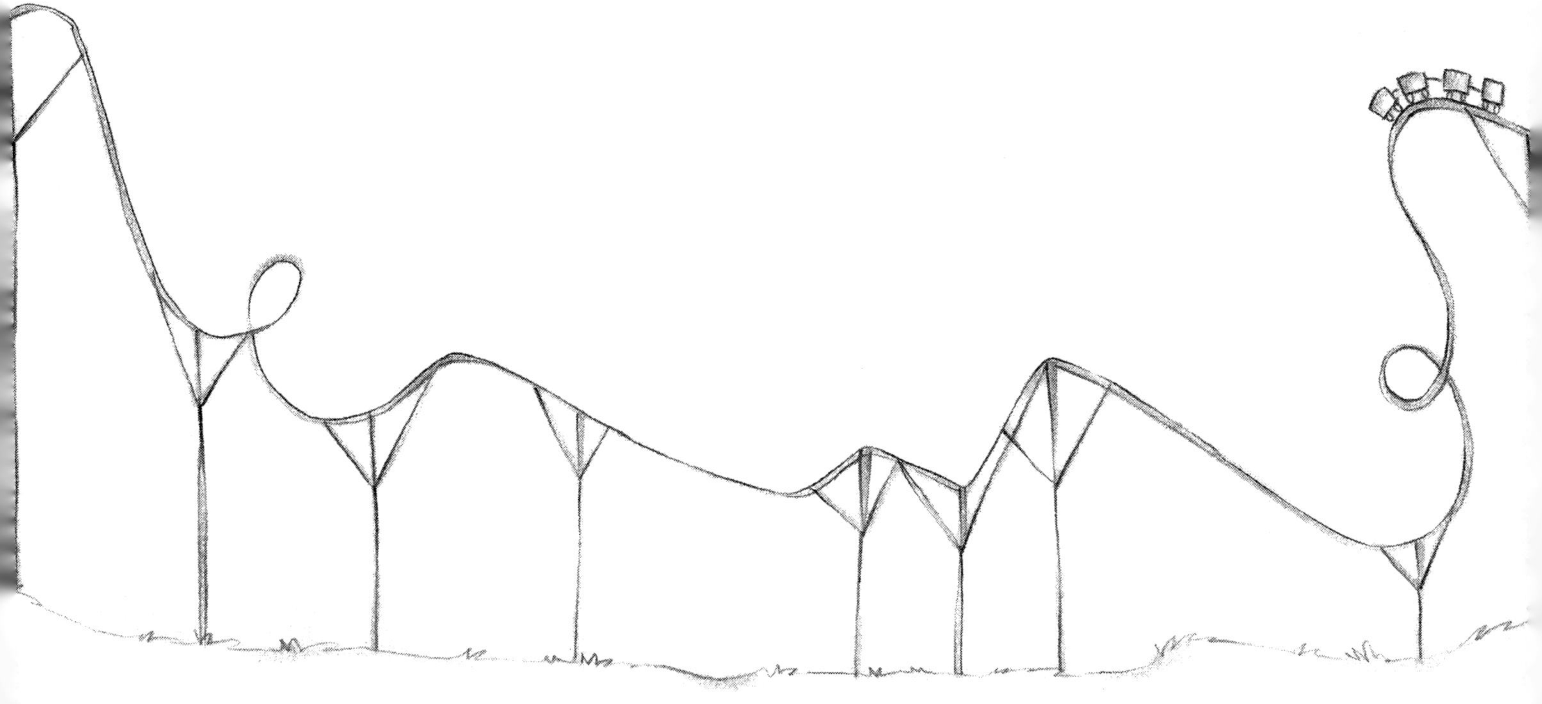

28016093R00016

Made in the USA
San Bernardino, CA
20 December 2015